Tax Strategies for Wealth Preservation

Preservation

A Comprehensive Guide

Table of Contents

1. Introduction 1

2. Understanding the Basics of Taxation 2

    2.1. Understanding Tax Structures 2

    2.2. Types of Taxes 2

    2.3. Taxation and Legal Entities 3

    2.4. Understanding Tax Liability 3

    2.5. Planning for Taxes 4

3. Introduction to Wealth Preservation 5

    3.1. The Fundamentals of Wealth Preservation 5

    3.2. The Role of Taxation in Wealth Preservation 6

    3.3. Crafting Your Tax Strategies 6

    3.4. The Complexity of Tax Laws 7

    3.5. Navigating the Tax Labyrinth 7

4. Integrating Tax Strategies into Your Financial Plan 9

    4.1. Understanding Your Current Financial Situation 9

    4.2. Developing a Tax Planning Strategy 9

    4.3. Choosing Tax-Advantaged Investment Vehicles 10

    4.4. Practicing Tax Loss Harvesting 10

    4.5. Exploring Estate Planning Techniques 10

    4.6. Employing Smart Generosity 11

    4.7. Leveraging Tax Credits 11

5. The Role of Retirement Accounts in Wealth Preservation 12

    5.1. Advantages of Tax-Deferred Retirement Accounts 12

    5.2. Types of Retirement Accounts 12

    5.3. Maximizing the Tax Advantages of Retirement Accounts 13

    5.4. The Power of Diversification 14

6. Real Estate and Tax Advantages: Leverage for Wealth
Conservation 15

6.1. Key Tax Advantages in Real Estate 15

6.2. Understanding Depreciation 16

6.3. Profiting from 1031 Exchange 16

6.4. Reaping the Benefits of Rental Income 17

6.5. Navigating Capital Gains Exclusion 17

7. Capital Gains and Losses: A Strategic Approach 19

7.1. Understanding Capital Gains and Losses 19

7.2. Capital Gains Tax Brackets 19

7.3. Tax-loss Harvesting 20

7.4. The Role of Tax-Deferred Accounts 20

7.5. Capital Gains and Real Estate 21

8. Charitable Gifts and Legacy Planning: Tax Implications 22

8.1. Charitable Donations: Understanding the Basics 22

8.2. Itemizing Deductions: A Crucial Decision 22

8.3. Donating Appreciated Assets: A Win-Win 23

8.4. Qualified Charitable Distributions: An Option for the

Retirees 23

8.5. Charitable Remainder Trusts and Charitable Lead Trusts . . . 24

8.6. Estate Tax and Inheritance Tax: The Role of Charitable

Giving 24

9. Income Shifting: A Method to Lower Your Tax Burden 26

9.1. The Theory of Income Shifting 26

9.2. The Mechanism of Income Shifting 26

9.3. Income Shifting to Family Members 27

9.4. Income Shifting to Businesses and Trusts 27

9.5. Strategic Asset Transfer 28

9.6. The International Perspective 28

9.7. Expert Guidance 28

9.8. Wrapping Up 29

10. Business Ownership: Exploring Potential Tax Deductions 30

10.1. Identifying Common Business Deductions 30

10.2. Hidden Gems: Not-So-Common Deductions 31

10.3. Making the Most of Your Deductions 31

10.4. A Closer Look: Depreciation 32

10.5. Avoiding Audit Traps 33

11. Future-Proofing Your Wealth: Tax Strategies for a Changing
Landscape 34

11.1. Understanding the Landscape 34

11.2. Strategies for Individuals............................ 34

11.3. Strategies for Families 35

11.4. Strategies for Businesses 35

11.5. Staying Informed.................................... 35

11.6. In Conclusion 36

Chapter 1. Introduction

Navigating the labyrinthine maze of tax laws can be a daunting endeavor, but it is an indispensable aspect of wealth preservation. Our Special Report, "Tax Strategies for Wealth Preservation: A Comprehensive Guide," is designed as your invaluable roadmap through this complex landscape. Written with clarity and precision, this guide aims to provide you with valuable insights, up-to-date methods, and advanced strategies to minimize your tax liability and achieve your financial objectives. By demystifying the technical jargons and delivering the intricate world of taxes in a down-to-earth manner, this report ushers you onto the path of informed financial decisions, thereby fostering your wealth protection and growth. A read through the first few pages will compel you to invest in this insightful guide, securing your financial future from excessive tax impositions.

Chapter 2. Understanding the Basics of Taxation

Taxation, at its core, is the system established by governments to finance public goods and services. It is a multi-leveled structure pivoting on the principle of wealth redistribution, enabling fiscal policies that often include an empathetic view towards societal needs.

2.1. Understanding Tax Structures

Every country has its unique tax structure designed according to the nation's social welfare needs, economic condition, and numerous socio-political considerations. Nevertheless, there are two basic tax structures followed globally - Progressive and Regressive.

1. **Progressive Taxation:** Under this structure, individuals with higher income pay a larger percent of their income in taxes compared to those with less. The intent is to redistribute wealth, promoting a more equitable society.

2. **Regressive Taxation:** As opposed to the progressive system, regressive taxation imposes a higher proportionate burden on those with lower income. For instance, sales tax is often viewed as regressive as it applies uniformly regardless of an individual's income.

2.2. Types of Taxes

Taxation varies in assessment and collection modes. Below are some commonly recognized forms of taxes:

1. **Income Tax:** Levied on individuals or entities, this tax is based on the taxpayer's income level or profits.

2. **Corporation Tax:** Imposed on the profits generated by businesses or corporations.

3. **Sales Tax:** Tax paid for goods and services at the point of sale. The end consumer usually bears this tax.

4. **Estate Tax:** Also known as inheritance tax, levied on an individual's estate after their death.

5. **Capital Gains Tax:** It's a tax on profits from the sale of a capital asset, like stocks or real estate.

6. **Property Tax:** A wealth tax on the assessed value of real estate owned by an individual or organization.

2.3. Taxation and Legal Entities

Individuals, corporations, trusts, and other entities are taxed differently, which can significantly impact wealth distribution and preservation. It is crucial to understand these differences when planning wealth preservation or estate planning strategies. Entities like trusts can provide substantial benefits, protecting assets from creditors and potentially reducing estate tax liability.

2.4. Understanding Tax Liability

A critical aspect of tax planning is determining one's tax liability, calculated by applying the relevant tax rate to the taxable income. Considerations such as deductions, credits, and exemptions play a crucial role in determining this liability.

1. **Deductions:** These reduce the amount of income subject to tax. Standard deductions include mortgage interest, educational expenses, certain business expenses, etc.

2. **Credits:** These directly reduce the tax bill. They can include credits for education costs, energy efficiency improvements, or for adoption, among others.

3. **Exemptions:** These reduce taxable income based on how many people are financially dependent on the taxpayer. However, the Tax Cuts and Jobs Act of 2017 has currently suspended personal exemptions.

2.5. Planning for Taxes

The key to reducing tax liability lies in tax planning. This process involves analyzing one's financial situation from a tax-efficiency perspective. Given this, strategic tax planning involves the consideration of when to incur income or expenses, the types of investments that provide preferable tax rates, and the kind of tax-saving retirement plans to employ.

It is vital to note that tax laws are dynamic, and multiple factors can influence legislation, such as political power shifts or economic circumstances. Therefore, what constitutes efficient tax planning in the current year may not be the same in the subsequent years.

One should also keep in mind the ethical implications while tax planning. While it's legal and beneficial to minimize tax burden by exploiting existing tax laws, aggressive tax avoidance can lead to legal implications.

In conclusion, understanding taxation basics is fundamental to effective wealth preservation strategies. It allows one to make informed decisions, reduce tax liabilities, and steer clear from unnecessary legal implications. Remember, understanding the basics is the first step towards becoming a proficient navigator through the confusing maze of tax laws.

Chapter 3. Introduction to Wealth Preservation

Wealth preservation is not a concept exclusive to financial gurus or successful entrepreneurs. It is a universal principle that every individual with any form of wealth, irrespective of its size, would benefit greatly from understanding. In its simplest essence, wealth preservation is the art and science of maintaining and growing one's wealth against the erosive forces of inflation, market volatility, and most notably, taxes.

3.1. The Fundamentals of Wealth Preservation

Wealth preservation can be envisioned as positioning your hard-earned wealth in the best possible way to withstand the impacts of economic and financial storm surges. But first, we must recognize that wealth is not just about money, real estate or shares. It could also incorporate your intellectual properties, arts, antiques, businesses, and various other assets which can serve as sources of income or repositories of value.

The heart of wealth preservation lies in balancing growth and safeguarding, ensuring that assets are not only growing but also protected against potential losses. To do this effectively, a broad understanding of economic trends, investment opportunities, and potential pitfalls is essential. Furthermore, the ability to adapt and strategize according to evolving circumstances and rules is a decisive factor in wealth longevity.

3.2. The Role of Taxation in Wealth Preservation

Taxation is an integral aspect of any wealth preservation strategy. While most discussions around wealth preservation center on the choice of investments, portfolio diversification, wealth transfer, and insurance coverage, the impact of taxation often receives the shrift. However, taxes – given their broad reach, vast applicability, and substantial rates – could shape, challenge, and even imperil wealth preservation goals in ways that few other factors can.

Understanding tax laws and leveraging legal opportunities to minimize tax liability can dramatically improve both wealth preservation and accumulation. Moreover, being unaware of the tax implications of your decisions can result in unintended tax liabilities, undermining your wealth.

3.3. Crafting Your Tax Strategies

Crafting your tax strategies begins with the understanding of your personal circumstances – your income sources, your liabilities, your current and future obligations, your lifestyle needs, your health, and your long-term goals. Once you've got a handle on where you stand and where you plan to go, the process of mapping out your tax strategies can begin.

Keep in mind that operating in unfamiliar terrain, such as the realm of tax law, is fraught with risks and potential pitfalls. Be prepared to seek out tax professionals, financial advisors, or wealth management experts to help you navigate these waters.

The need to evolve your strategies as your situation changes cannot be overstated. Changes in personal financial status, shifts in the broader economic landscape, new tax laws or amendments to existing ones — each can require a recalibration of your tax strategies.

3.4. The Complexity of Tax Laws

As one navigates the labyrinth of taxation, it becomes formidable to keep track of all the variables, laws, amendments, and relevant court verdicts. Knowing how your local, state, federal, and international taxes work, and interacting with each other, can seem like an insurmountable challenge. Besides, each form of wealth carries its specific tax implications, making the project more intricate.

However, the key to successful wealth preservation is not letting the potential complexity of tax laws intimidate you. Think of them as codes to be cracked, riddles to be solved — and rest assured that with the right help, every code is crackable, every riddle is solvable.

3.5. Navigating the Tax Labyrinth

Throughout the guide, we will take a closer look at various tax rules, how they could affect you, and strategies to minimize your tax liabilities. It will include building blocks of effective tax strategies, such as understanding tax deductions and credits, using retirement accounts, gift and estate planning, capital gains tax management, property tax understanding, and turning charitable goals into tax savings opportunities.

We will also discuss advanced tax techniques, like tax loss harvesting, tax-efficient investing and withdrawal strategies, setting up trusts and tax-exempt entities, leveraging tax treaties, and incorporating tax-friendly jurisdictions for certain forms of wealth.

Remember, wealth preservation, just like wealth accumulation, isn't something that happens overnight. It is a journey that you embark upon, step by step, decision by decision, and along the way, knowledge is your most trusted ally. The strategies and insights in the following chapters are aimed at aiding you in this journey. This way, you'll become adept at understanding and using tax strategies not just for preserving your wealth, but to flourish it.

Embrace the journey, and let's begin.

Chapter 4. Integrating Tax Strategies into Your Financial Plan

Integrating tax strategies into your financial plan is a multifaceted process covering several important areas. Below, we will delve into the details, providing a thorough overview of how you can make the tax code work to your advantage.

4.1. Understanding Your Current Financial Situation

The first step in integrating tax strategies into your financial plan is to fully understand your current financial situation. You need to have a clear view of your income (and its sources), your expenses, your assets, and your liabilities. Also, you must be aware of the tax benefits or burdens linked to these aspects.

A key point of focus should be the type of taxable income you possess. Are you earning income through regular employment, self-employment, investment dividends, royalties, etc.? Each of these sources of income has different tax implications and, thus, requires a tailored tax strategy.

4.2. Developing a Tax Planning Strategy

With a comprehensive understanding of your finances, you can now develop a tax planning strategy that suits your needs. Every financial decision has a tax consequence, so proactive planning is vital. This strategy should involve timing income and expenses, size and structure of investments, selection of tax-advantaged accounts, and more.

For example, timing income and expenses could involve deciding whether to take a bonus in December or January, based on which year it would be more tax-efficient. The size and structure of investments would affect your capital gains tax, and the selection of tax-advantaged accounts determines how your retirement savings would be taxed.

4.3. Choosing Tax-Advantaged Investment Vehicles

There are various investment vehicles designed to provide tax advantages. The most common include retirement accounts like 401(k)s and IRAs, education savings accounts like 529 plans, and health savings accounts. Each of these accommodates different life expenses, but they all share a common characteristic: they have distinct tax advantages. For example, contributions to a 401(k) are tax-deductible, growth in a 529 plan is tax-free, and withdrawals from an HSA for qualified medical expenses are also tax-free.

4.4. Practicing Tax Loss Harvesting

Tax loss harvesting is a crucial strategy for reducing your tax liability. This entails selling losing investments to offset the taxable gain from successful ones. Although you're realizing a loss, the silver lining is that this loss will reduce your overall tax liability.

4.5. Exploring Estate Planning Techniques

Estate planning has considerable tax implications, especially for high-net-worth individuals. Through tools like trusts and gifts, you can minimize the amount of your estate that will get eaten up by taxes. However, it's critical to remember these strategies require careful planning and are best conducted under the advice of an estate planning specialist.

4.6. Employing Smart Generosity

Aligning your financial plan with charitable goals can yield significant tax benefits. The charitable contribution deduction allows you to receive a tax deduction for contributions made to qualified charitable organizations. This can also include gifting appreciated securities, which would allow you to avoid capital gains tax on those securities.

4.7. Leveraging Tax Credits

Tax credits are a powerful tool for reducing your overall tax liability. Be aware of the tax credits you qualify for, such as the Child Tax Credit, the Earned Income Tax Credit, or the American Opportunity Credit. Each of these can provide substantial savings on your tax bill.

By implementing these strategies into your financial plan, you can work towards not only preserving your wealth but also growing it over time. With careful planning and a comprehensive understanding of your financial picture, you can navigate the tax landscape and achieve your financial goals.

Chapter 5. The Role of Retirement Accounts in Wealth Preservation

From the early stages of your career to the moment you hang up your work boots, your financial decisions play a vital role in determining your wealth accumulation journey. Retirement accounts hold a strategic position in this journey, offering not just a source of income in your golden years, but also an excellent instrument for wealth preservation and growth. Utilizing these accounts with an understanding of their tax benefits doesn't just save money but helps in wealth accumulation.

5.1. Advantages of Tax-Deferred Retirement Accounts

Tax-deferred retirement accounts, like a 401(k) or an Individual Retirement Account (IRA), offer significant tax advantages. In these accounts, your contributions are typically 'pre-tax' or tax-deductible, meaning they effectively reduce your taxable income for the year you contribute.

In addition, the funds in a tax-deferred retirement account grow tax-free until you make a withdrawal, which is typically during retirement when you may be in a lower tax bracket. This principle of deferral allows your retirement funds to compound over time, offering potentially far greater returns than a taxable account.

5.2. Types of Retirement Accounts

There are several types of retirement accounts available, each with its own set of benefits and rules.

401(k): A defined-contribution plan offered by employers. Employees can contribute a portion of their pre-tax salary, which is then often matched by the employer. No taxes are paid on the funds until they are withdrawn at retirement.

Individual Retirement Account (IRA): Comes in two forms - Traditional and Roth. Traditional IRAs are tax-deferred, while Roth IRAs are funded with after-tax money, and withdrawals are tax-free in retirement.

SEP IRA: A simplified employee pension (SEP IRA) allows self-employed individuals and small business owners to make tax-deductible contributions toward their own and their employees' retirement.

Solo 401(k): Available to self-employed individuals with no employees. The Solo 401(k) allows for high contribution levels and can be set up as a traditional or a Roth account.

5.3. Maximizing the Tax Advantages of Retirement Accounts

You can preserve a significant portion of your wealth by fully utilizing the tax advantages of retirement accounts. Here are some strategies that you might consider:

1. Maximize your contributions: Retirement accounts have annual contribution limits. In a 401(k), for example, as of 2021, you can contribute up to $19,500, or $26,000 if you're age 50 or older. Maxing out your contributions allows you to reduce your taxable income to the greatest extent possible.

2. Employ catch-up contributions: If you're age 50 or older, you're allowed to make additional contributions to your retirement

accounts - these are called 'catch-up' contributions. This can be a powerful way to boost your retirement savings and preserve your wealth.

3. Roll-overs: Should you change jobs or have multiple retirement accounts, a roll-over can help avoid early withdrawal penalties and continue the tax-advantaged growth of your funds.

4. Tax-efficient withdrawal: It's critical to strategize your withdrawal to minimize the tax impact, which includes contemplating the timing and the amount. If possible, staying in the lower tax bracket even in retirement can help reduce your total tax liability.

5.4. The Power of Diversification

Having multiple retirement accounts can provide a greater measure of control over tax liabilities in retirement. By diversifying between taxable, tax-deferred (traditional 401(k) or IRA), and tax-free accounts (Roth 401(k) or Roth IRA), you can choose which funds to withdraw from each year to manage your tax situation.

Remember, tax laws and annual limits can change, and there can be penalties for withdrawing funds early or contributing too much. It's essential always to stay updated with the changes and liaise with your financial advisor to ensure optimal wealth preservation strategies.

Indeed, the proper use of retirement accounts can significantly impact your wealth preservation efforts. They are not mere savings containers but powerful tools that, when maximized, provide significant wealth protection and growth opportunities. The compound interest accrued over time in these tax-beneficial accounts can lead to substantial wealth accumulation, fortifying your financial future.

Chapter 6. Real Estate and Tax Advantages: Leverage for Wealth Conservation

Real estate, the quiet anchor in any robust portfolio, offers a unique amalgamation of benefits over other investment channels, making it an excellent contender for wealth conservation. The beauty of real estate lies not only in its appreciation potential but significantly within its interaction with the emblematic complexities of tax norms. Hence, understanding how these tax advantages come into play can be a game-changer for your wealth preservation strategy.

6.1. Key Tax Advantages in Real Estate

The Internal Revenue Service (IRS) provides several tax benefits for real estate investors, which are instrumental in preserving and enhancing wealth. Some of the significant advantages include:

1. Deductions on Mortgage Interest: Mortgage interest, involving interest paid on a loan secured by a main or secondary home, is essentially deductible in most instances.

2. Property Tax Deduction: Real estate tax imposed on your primary or secondary home, or other properties you own, can usually be deducted.

3. Depreciation: This unique advantage lets you recover the cost of an income-producing property through yearly tax deductions, spreading this across the lifespan of the property.

4. Rental Income Taxation: Rental income is not subject to self-employment tax and, coupled with deductible expenses, might result in no tax obligation.

5. Capital Gains Exclusion: Allowances are made for homeowners who sell their primary residence, with single filers excluding up to $250,000, and married filers, $500,000 of gains, from taxes.

6. 1031 Exchange: This provision enables investors to postpone paying taxes on gains from selling an investment property, given they reinvest the proceeds into a property of 'like-kind'.

Let's delve deeper into some of these advantages in order to create a more cogent picture of the tax benefits within the realm of real estate.

6.2. Understanding Depreciation

Depreciation is one of the cornerstones of tax benefits in real estate, with such significance ascribed to this tax advantage because it allows a deduction without an actual expense of cash during the year. This generally results in a paper loss that might offset other types of income on your tax return.

The IRS typically allows real estate investors to deduct the price of investment properties over a span of 27.5 years for residential properties and 39 years for commercial properties. This steady, yearly deduction can significantly deflate your tax liability, providing an apt trajectory for wealth conservation.

6.3. Profiting from 1031 Exchange

While the typical ethos of investment directs one to sell high after buying low, such a strategy in the world of real estate could lead to a hefty tax bill on your capital gains. This is where a 1031 Exchange can be a potent tool for wealth preservation.

A 1031 Exchange allows an investor to sell a property and reinvest the proceeds in a new, 'like-kind' property, deferring all capital gain taxes. This tactic is exceptional in maximizing the power of your investment dollar. Effectively, it allows the 'profit' from a sale to be used fully for reinvestment without being minimalized by taxes.

It's vital, however, to navigate the rules governing 1031 Exchanges carefully, as inappropriate application can result in severe tax consequences.

6.4. Reaping the Benefits of Rental Income

Rental income serves as a stable income stream, often higher than dividends from investments of similar risk levels. What makes it even more attractive from a tax standpoint is its exclusion from self-employment tax. Furthermore, expenses originating from managing and maintaining the rental property are deductible, providing further diminishments to your tax obligation.

However, it's pertinent to keep in mind that excess losses might not be fully deductible due to the IRS Passive Activity Loss restrictions. Understanding the rules surrounding these can be pivotal in optimizing your rental income benefits.

6.5. Navigating Capital Gains Exclusion

Capital Gains Exclusion on the sale of your home is a significant boon to legal residents, as it allows for the exclusion of a hefty sum from capital gains taxes (up to $250,000 for single and $500,000 for married couples filing jointly). It requires living in and owning the home for 2 of the 5 years before the sale.

Remember, though, that laws periodically change, and any changes to this provision might impact your strategy, showcasing the importance of regular updates from a reliable tax advisor.

This comprehensive review of the tax advantages within real estate investing should offer a solid foundation from which you can start to build your wealth preservation strategy. A sound understanding of these benefits will equip you to capitalize on opportunities and guard your wealth effectively.

However, keep in mind that tax laws are intricate and have many subtleties. Therefore, it's advisable to partner with a knowledgeable tax advisor to ensure compliance while still taking full advantage of these benefits to preserve and grow your wealth.

Chapter 7. Capital Gains and Losses: A Strategic Approach

In understanding the landscape of wealth preservation, one cannot overlook the significance of capital gains and losses considerations. This section provides an encyclopedic overview, delving deep into the strategies for managing these gains and losses to your advantage.

7.1. Understanding Capital Gains and Losses

Let us first begin by conceptualizing capital gains and losses. At a fundamental level, a capital gain transpires when a capital asset - which could be stocks, bonds, precious metals, real estate, or other investments - is sold for a price above its original cost basis. Conversely, a capital loss occurs when the sale price is less than the cost basis.

However, the concept is not simply confined to the precipice of buy-low, sell-high. Inclusions such as dividends, interest payments, rentals, and royalties also factor into determining the capital gains. The confluence of these factors leads to the complexity of capital gains management.

7.2. Capital Gains Tax Brackets

Capital gains taxes introduce an added intricacy to this mix. For a simplistic perspective, capital gains can be divided into short-term and long-term. If you hold an asset for a year or less before selling, the gain will be considered a short-term capital gain, which is subject to taxation at your regular income tax level.

On the other hand, holding the asset for over a year welcomes a long-term capital gains status. These gains will face the wrath of taxation at a lower rate, depending on your taxable income. It is worthwhile to note that long-term capital gains tax rates are generally more favorable, providing incentive for long-term investment.

Understanding this taxonomy of capital gains taxes and their associated brackets is a necessary precursor for strategic navigation.

7.3. Tax-loss Harvesting

An essential strategy for managing capital gains and losses is Tax-Loss Harvesting (TLH). This strategy involves selling off securities at a loss to offset a capital gains tax liability. The critical aspect here is the notion of 'wash sale rule'. This rule prevents you from claiming a tax benefit from a loss on the sale of a security and then buying a significantly identical stock or security within a 30-day timeframe prior or post the sale.

Armed with the knowledge of this rule, you can strategically plan sales of assets and simultaneous investments. It's a delicate balance to tread, making sure you are not violating the 'wash sale' rule and yet accentuating your tax benefits.

7.4. The Role of Tax-Deferred Accounts

Equally important in the strategic approach to capital gains and losses are tax-deferred accounts. As the name implies, these accounts provide a deferral mechanism for payment of taxes. Examples of tax-deferred accounts include individual retirement accounts (IRAs) and 401(k) plans. These accounts allow for investments to grow tax-free until withdrawn.

However, bear in mind the restrictions imposed on these accounts, such as penalties on early withdrawals or specific contribution limits.

It is essential to understand these rules thoroughly in order to maximize your benefits.

7.5. Capital Gains and Real Estate

Investing in real estate also provides its own host of special rules and opportunities. For instance, the section 1031 exchange, or a 'like-kind' exchange, allows you to defer paying capital gains taxes when you sell an investment property and reinvest the proceeds from the sale within specific time limits in a property or properties of like-kind and equal or greater value.

In addition, there is the home sale exclusion, that allows you to exclude up to $250,000 ($500,000 if you're married and file jointly) of gain on the sale of your primary home if you meet a certain set of requirements.

In conclusion, understanding the landscape of capital gains and losses is a strategic endeavor, one that requires the wielding of complex tax codes and laws to your advantage. Whether it's about understanding tax brackets, engaging in tax-loss harvesting, using tax-deferred accounts, or navigating real estate investments, every aspect can be leveraged to protect your wealth from excessive taxation.

Chapter 8. Charitable Gifts and Legacy Planning: Tax Implications

The philanthropic act of charitable giving not only benefits the recipient organization but is often accompanied by significant tax advantages for the donor. Leveraging these benefits is a strategic aspect in wealth preservation and legacy planning, requiring a clear understanding and prudent implementation.

8.1. Charitable Donations: Understanding the Basics

Tax laws governing charitable donations are intricate and loaded with caveats. However, a basic understanding lays a foundation to exploit opportunities while avoiding pitfalls. Donations to registered non-profit organizations (501(c)(3) in the US) are generally tax-deductible. These deductions can offset your income, potentially pushing you into a lower tax bracket and reducing your overall tax liability.

Perhaps the famous quote by Jean-Baptiste Colbert, "The art of taxation consists in so plucking the goose as to obtain the largest amount of feathers with the least amount of hissing," best describes the conundrum of taxation. With strategic planning and the right dose of philanthropy, the tax pinch can somewhat be ameliorated.

8.2. Itemizing Deductions: A Crucial Decision

The decision whether to take the standard deduction or itemize on your tax return is vital. Taxpayers can deduct the amount they give to charity, but to do this, they must itemize. With changes brought about by the Tax Cuts and Jobs Act (TCJA), more taxpayers may find the larger standard deduction more beneficial.

However, if you choose to itemize, it is essential to keep accurate records of all charitable donations. These include both cash and non-cash donations, such as stocks and property. The IRS requires documented proof in case of an audit, so be sure to obtain and retain donation receipts.

8.3. Donating Appreciated Assets: A Win-Win

Donating appreciated assets like stocks and mutual funds offers a dual advantage. Not only can you claim the full fair-market value as a charitable deduction, but you also avoid the capital gains tax that would arise from selling these assets. It's an opportunity to do good while benefiting your bottom line.

8.4. Qualified Charitable Distributions: An Option for the Retirees

If you are 70½ years or older and have an Individual Retirement Account (IRA), you can make a Qualified Charitable Distribution (QCD) directly from your IRA to a qualified charity. This can count towards satisfying your required minimum distributions (RMDs) and won't be included in your taxable income, potentially reducing the income and taxes on your Social Security benefits and Medicare premiums.

8.5. Charitable Remainder Trusts and Charitable Lead Trusts

Charitable Remainder Trusts (CRTs) and Charitable Lead Trusts (CLTs) are advanced strategies available for gifting large amounts to charities. A CRT allows you to make a donation, take an immediate tax deduction, and receive income from the trust for life or a specified period. Upon termination, the remaining assets go to the charity.

Conversely, a CLT pays income to a charity for a set period, and the remaining assets go to your beneficiaries, often with reduced estate taxes. Both strategies allow donors to make significant charitable donations while providing for their financial needs or those of their designated beneficiaries.

8.6. Estate Tax and Inheritance Tax: The Role of Charitable Giving

Another advantage of charitable giving deserves mention in the context of estate planning: the potential reduction of estate taxes. Bequests to charities are generally exempt from estate tax, thus reducing the size of your taxable estate. Likewise, gifts to charities can mitigate potential inheritance tax implications.

In conclusion, charitable gifts offer an effective avenue for wealth preservation and legacy planning. Their tax implications necessitate a nuanced understanding of the underlying laws. Therefore, consulting with a financial advisor or a tax professional can help optimize your gifting strategies in line with your overall financial goals. The wisdom of Deepak Chopra, who observed that "wealth, in fact, is a mindset," succinctly marshals the essence: the right mindset, fortified by knowledge and strategic planning, can navigate the tax labyrinth to preserve one's wealth.

(Note: The U.S tax laws serve as the reference for this chapter. The codes and its interpretations can change, and the applicability can vary depending on individual circumstances. Always seek professional advice before making any financial or tax-related decisions.)

Chapter 9. Income Shifting: A Method to Lower Your Tax Burden

Income shifting is a strategic method employed to manage, reduce, and control tax liabilities. Under this method, income is moved from a high-tax entity, person, or jurisdiction to a lower one. This technique, while perfectly legal, is complex and requires a deft understanding and proper application to avoid regulatory pitfalls and ensure operational efficiency.

9.1. The Theory of Income Shifting

The concept of income shifting is rooted in the differential tax status and rates applicable to various entities, people, and jurisdictions. Exploiting these disparities can result in substantial tax savings. For instance, if a business owner who is in a higher tax bracket can strategically shift profits to a family member in a lower tax bracket, overall taxes can be significantly reduced.

However, tax law is static and focuses not only on the letter but the spirit of the law. Therefore, understanding and conforming to the underlying principles of tax codes are critical. Income and assets must be shifted in a manner that adheres strictly to domestic and international tax laws.

9.2. The Mechanism of Income Shifting

Income shifting involves several key steps, each of which is crucial to the overall effectiveness of the strategy.

1. Identify potential recipients: Eligible recipients of income shifting include family members or other entities in lower tax brackets.

2. Create a legitimate avenue for income shifting: This might involve employing a family member or incorporating a lower-tax jurisdiction entity.

3. Shift income: The high-tax entity or individual may then shift income to the chosen recipient, typically in the form of wages, dividends, or interest.

9.3. Income Shifting to Family Members

Imbuing wealth to younger family members in lower tax brackets can have notable benefits. Yet, specific regulations must be observed especially when minor recipients are concerned.

Minor children can earn a specific amount annually without incurring federal income tax. However, "kiddie tax" regulations might affect unearned income above a set limit. Wages or other earned income are not subject to these rules, which makes legitimate employment a productive method to shift income.

In order to comply with the relevant laws, such employment needs to be genuine and the wages reasonable for the work performed. Meticulous documentation is necessary to back the legitimacy of the work relationship and wage levels.

9.4. Income Shifting to Businesses and Trusts

Income can also be shifted to lower-tax businesses or trusts. Shifting income to a C corporation, for instance, enables profits to be taxed at the corporate rate, typically lower than the personal tax rate. Income can be further shifted to shareholders by way of dividends.

However, careful planning is advised before shifting income to corporations as "double taxation" can sometimes occur. That's where the income gets taxed twice - once at the corporate level and again upon distribution to shareholders.

Trusts can be another destination for shifting income. By transferring income-generating assets into a trust, income can be moved to beneficiaries in lower tax brackets.

9.5. Strategic Asset Transfer

The transfer of assets is often a noteworthy step in income shifting. High-income individuals or businesses might consider transferring income-generating properties to those in lower tax brackets.

Before initiating such moves, be wary of the possible drawbacks. Some transferred assets' appreciated value may be subjected to tax, potentially negating the tax savings gained from income shifting.

9.6. The International Perspective

Turning to jurisdictions with lower tax rates is a common way to engage in income shifting. However, adhering to the legalities of international taxation is crucial. The OECD's BEPS (Base Erosion and Profit Shifting) initiatives aim to combat tax avoidance strategies that exploit gaps and mismatches in tax rules. Compliance with international regulations is essential to mitigate the risk of penalties or reputational damage.

9.7. Expert Guidance

To implement income shifting strategies effectively and legitimately, professional advice is a must. Tax law is a dynamic and complex field; non-compliance - intentional or inadvertent - can lead to penalties and legal issues.

9.8. Wrapping Up

Even though income shifting can be an effective method to reduce tax burdens, it must be carefully planned and executed. A basic tenet to remember is that any action taken should have a sound economic or business purpose beyond merely reducing tax. By ensuring these strategies' legality, income shifting can play a central role in wealth preservation and financial planning strategy.

Chapter 10. Business Ownership: Exploring Potential Tax Deductions

Exploring the myriad tax deductions available to business owners is a crucial element in smarter tax planning and wealth preservation. The ability to identify, understand, and strategically employ these deductions can lead to significant reductions in the liabilities burdened by your business, ultimately driving up net profits.

10.1. Identifying Common Business Deductions

Business deductions operate under the premise that any expense incurred in the earning of business income can be deducted from the gross income of that business, typically reducing taxable income. Here are some common business expenses you might deduct:

1. Operating costs: These encompass any costs related to the general running of the business — rent, utilities, office supplies, and the like.

2. Salaries and wages: As long as they are reasonable, salaries paid to employees and to yourself are tax-deductible.

3. Travel expenses: Luckily for globe-trotters, travel expenses for business purposes are among the costs that can be deducted.

4. Legal and professional fees: Professional fees paid to attorneys, tax professionals, and consultants can be written off.

5. Communications: Phone, internet costs, and other communication utilities are also deductible.

6. Depreciation: Depreciation on assets like buildings, machinery,

equipment, furniture, and some intangible properties can also be deducted.

Many business owners underutilize these deductions due to the intimidating complexity that can arise when understanding tax laws. Without proper documentation or understanding, they risk attracting unwanted attention from tax authorities.

10.2. Hidden Gems: Not-So-Common Deductions

While most businesses are well-versed in the common business deductions, they often miss the not-so-obvious ones. Some of these lesser-known yet equally important deductions include:

1. Software and subscriptions: Software required for business operations and relevant industry subscriptions can be written off.

2. Banking fees: Any fees associated with business bank accounts are deductible.

3. Business insurance: Premiums paid for business insurance are tax-deductible too.

4. Training and education: Any education or training provided for the betterment of your employees can be an expense deduction.

5. Home office: If a part of your home acts as your primary place of business, you're eligible for the home office deduction.

10.3. Making the Most of Your Deductions

Strategic planning allows business owners to maximize their deductions. To achieve this, keep the following in mind:

1. Organize and keep track of all business expenses as they occur. This will lessen the burden come tax time and ensure accuracy in your reports. Use of accounting software can make this task easier.

2. Time large purchases and expenses to offset high-revenue years. Some expenses may need to be spread out over several tax years under depreciation rules. Consult with a tax professional to plan these decisions appropriately.

3. Review the tax code each year for updates and changes to deductions. Tax laws change regularly, and new deductions may become available.

10.4. A Closer Look: Depreciation

Depreciation is perhaps one of the most overlooked and misunderstood deductions. In short, depreciation lets business owners deduct the costs of certain assets over time. While the concept may sound simple, it gets complicated quickly once you factor in rules regarding different depreciation methods, property classes, and deduction limits.

The basic formula for depreciation is: Cost of the Business Asset / Useful Life of the Asset. Take, for example, an office computer worth $2,000 with a useful life of five years. In this case, you could deduct $400 each year for the next five years.

However, under certain tax laws like Section 179, business owners may be allowed to deduct the full cost of an asset in the year of its purchase, instead of spreading the deductions over the asset's lifespan. Again, it is crucial to consult with a tax professional to navigate through these exceptions.

10.5. Avoiding Audit Traps

With great deductions come great responsibilities. Being audited is a very real fear for most business owners, due to the time-consuming and costly process. Here's what can help you avoid an audit:

1. Only deduct legitimate business expenses and maintain a separate bank account for business transactions to avoid mingling personal and business expenses.

2. Keep accurate records of deductions, complete with receipts and the business reasons for the expenses.

3. Self-employment tax is an area where many business owners get into trouble with the IRS. If you are self-employed, you'll owe this tax over and above income tax. Hence, it is essential to understand and plan for it.

To summarize, understanding and managing tax deductions is an ongoing and strategic process and not just a once-a-year event. Tax-efficient business practices can deliver significant financial benefits, while oversight or missteps can lead to severe fiscal penalties. A proactive approach, coupled with knowledgeable tax advisors, can turn the labyrinth of tax laws into a navigational tool to steer your business and wealth towards growth and preservation.

[1]: IRS. (2020). Topic No. 509 Business Use of Car | Internal Revenue Service (U.S. Government). Retrieved from the official IRS website. [2]: IRS. (2020). Topic No. 514 Self-Employment Tax | Internal Revenue Service (U.S. Government). Retrieved from the official IRS website.

Chapter 11. Future-Proofing Your Wealth: Tax Strategies for a Changing Landscape

In a world where economic landscapes are constantly evolving, one of the central challenges in wealth preservation is to future-proof one's wealth against the shifting landscape of tax rules and obligations. By staying attuned to these shifts and being proactive in addressing them, it is possible to both protect and grow wealth over long term.

11.1. Understanding the Landscape

The first step in devising effective tax strategies is an in-depth understanding of the current tax environment and how it is expected to change over time. At a national level, this involves following the trajectory of tax law, gaining a sense of the general direction of policy reform, and being mindful of specific changes that could have a direct impact on one's wealth.

At an international level, the picture is even more complex. Trends such as the global exchange of tax information, increased transparency requirements, and clampdown on tax evasion demand careful attention.

11.2. Strategies for Individuals

The core principle in future-proofing wealth for individuals is maximizing tax-efficient methods of savings and investments. Utilizing tax-advantaged accounts, strategically timing income and expenses, and making the most of deductions and credits all play a vital role in protecting wealth.

Annuities, 401(k) accounts, and individual retirement accounts (IRA) can offer significant tax advantages. However, each has its own set of rules regarding contributions, withdrawals, and inheritance which can further influence the tax implications.

11.3. Strategies for Families

When it comes to protecting wealth within a family, estate planning and gift taxes become crucial areas to consider. Transfer of wealth within a family can attract significant tax liabilities, and strategies like trust funds, family limited partnerships, and gifting below the annual gift tax exclusion can help reduce this tax burden.

Inter-generational wealth transfer is another area that demands careful tax planning to avoid the decline in value due to tax liability. Advisory professionals specialized in these matters can offer a valuable perspective and guidance.

11.4. Strategies for Businesses

For business owners, corporate tax strategy becomes a key pillar in preserving wealth. As tax laws around corporations fluctuate, business structures should be regularly evaluated to ensure they are the most tax-efficient.

Considerations include whether to incorporate, how to handle retained earnings, and how to best manage capital gains and losses. Utilizing international tax treaties, geographic tax credits, and tax-efficient reinvestments can all serve to minimize tax liability.

11.5. Staying Informed

Keeping abreast of changes in tax laws, both domestically and abroad, is a necessity. Engaging the services of a tax consultant or wealth management advisor, joining relevant seminars, and subscribing to financial and tax journals can greatly assist in identifying and understanding major tax shifts.

11.6. In Conclusion

While the landscape of tax law may be challenging to navigate, employing these strategies can help you make informed, advantageous financial decisions. Future-proofing your wealth, though demanding vigilant attention and perspicacity, can ensure that the changing tides of tax laws won't erode your hard-earned wealth. With the right planning and advisory support, you can stay ahead of the curve, securing your assets and propelling your wealth growth into the future.

As we navigate this shifting landscape, the longstanding principles of tactical planning, informed decision-making, and prudent guidance persist. In essence, the keen understanding and strategic handling of tax regulations are pivotal in preserving and fostering wealth, further underscoring the importance of this pursuit.

www.ingramcontent.com/pod-product-compliance
Lightning Source LLC
Chambersburg PA
CBHW072223290526
45794CB00007B/2859